Recollections Of The Private Life Of Napoleon

Volume 1

by

Louis Constant Wairy

Double9 BOOKS

Recollections Of The Private Life Of Napoleon
Volume 1
by Louis Constant Wairy

ISBN: 978-93-76395-54-5

Published by

DOUBLE 9 BOOKS
2/13-B, Ansari Road
Daryaganj, New Delhi – 110002
info@double9books.com
www.double9books.com
Tel. 011-40042856

ABOUT THE AUTHOR

Louis Constant Wairy is portrayed as an individual whose life path was shaped by early upheaval, eventually leading to a role that placed him in close proximity to a significant leader whose public power contrasted with private complexity. His account reflects a commitment to documenting daily routines, personal habits, and human inconsistencies rather than repeating interpretations influenced by political agendas. Through years of service in an intimate position, he developed insights into the contrast between authority and vulnerability, observing how discipline, ambition, and emotional strain formed an intricate part of the environment surrounding this central figure. His writing emphasizes the value of firsthand experience, using small details and encounters to illuminate aspects of leadership that conventional histories often overlook. Instead of focusing solely on achievements, he highlights the subtler qualities that define private identity, creating a portrayal grounded in observation and shaped by the same tensions between power, responsibility, and humanity that resonate throughout the themes explored in the book.

CONTENTS

PREFACE

Though this work was first published in 1830, it has never before been translated into English. Indeed, the volumes are almost out of print. When in Paris a few years ago the writer secured, with much difficulty, a copy, from which this translation has been made. Notes have been added by the translator, and illustrations by the publishers, which, it is believed, will enhance the interest of the original work by Constant.

"To paint Caesar in undress is not to paint Caesar," some one has said. Yet men will always like to see the great 'en deshabille'. In these volumes the hero is painted in undress. His foibles, his peculiarities, his vices, are here depicted without reserve. But so also are his kindness of heart, his vast intellect, his knowledge of men, his extraordinary energy, his public spirit. The shutters are taken down, and the workings of the mighty machinery are laid bare.

The late Prince Napoleon (who was more truly "the nephew of his uncle" than was Napoleon III.), in his Napoleon and His Detractors, bitterly assails this work of Constants attacking both its authenticity and the correctness of its statements. But there appears no good reason to doubt its genuineness, and the truthfulness of many of its details is amply supported by other authorities. Notwithstanding its excesses and follies, the great French Revolution will ever have an absorbing interest for mankind, because it began as a struggle for the advancement of the cause of manhood, liberty, and equal rights. It was a terribly earnest movement; and, after the lapse of a century, interest continues unabated in the great soldier who restored order, and organized and preserved the new ideas by means of his Civil Code and a firm government.

Countless memoirs have been published by those who lived in those heroic times. Yet everything which will cast new light upon the chief actors in that great drama of humanity is still seized upon with avidity, especially whatever concerns the Emperor.

This is not merely because he was a great conqueror; for such were, after their fashion, Genghis Khan and Timour, and hundreds of others. But it is because of the human interest which attaches to the wonderful career of Napoleon and the events of which he was the central figure.

Never did poet or novelist imagine scenes so improbable. The son of an obscure lawyer in an unimportant island becomes Emperor of the French and King of Italy. His brothers and sisters become kings and queens. The sons of innkeepers, notaries; lawyers, and peasants become marshals of the empire. The Emperor, first making a West India Creole his wife and Empress, puts her away, and marries a daughter of the haughtiest and oldest royal house in Europe, the niece of a queen whom the people of France had beheaded a few years before. Their son is born a king—King of Rome. Then suddenly the pageantry dissolves, and Emperor, kings, and queens become subjects again. Has imagination ever dreamed anything wilder than this? The dramatic interest of this story will always attract, but there is a deeper one. The secret spring of all those rapid changes, and the real cause of the great interest humanity will always feel in the story of those eventful times, is to be found in Napoleon's own explanation—"A career open to talents, without distinction of birth." Till that day the accident of birth was the key to every honor and every position. No man could hold even a lieutenancy in the army who could not show four quarterings on his coat of arms.

It was as the "armed apostle of democracy" that Napoleon went forth conquering and to conquer. He declared at St. Helena that he "had always marched supported by the opinions of six millions of men."

The old woman who met him incognito climbing the hill of Tarare, and replying to his assertion that "Napoleon was only a tyrant like the rest," exclaimed, "It may be so, but the others are the kings of the nobility, while he is one of us, and we have chosen him ourselves," expressed a great truth. As long as Napoleon represented popular sovereignty he was invincible; but when, deeming himself strong enough to stand alone, he endeavored to conciliate the old order of things, and, divorcing the daughter of the people, took for a bride the daughter of kings and allied himself with them—at that moment, like another Samson, "his strength departed from him." Disasters came as they had come to him before, but this time the heart of the people was no longer with him. He fell.

This man has been studied as a soldier, a statesman, an organizer, a politician. In all he was undeniably great. But men will always like to know something about him as a man. Can he stand that ordeal? These volumes will answer that question. They are written by one who joined the First Consul at the Hospice on Mt. St. Bernard, on his way to Marengo, in June, 1800, and who was with him as his chief personal attendant, day and night, never leaving him "any more than his shadow" (eight days only) excepted until that eventful day, fourteen years later, when, laying aside the sceptre of the greatest empire the world had known for seventeen centuries, he walked down the horseshoe steps at Fontainebleau in the presence of the soldiers whom he had led to victory from Madrid to Moscow, once more a private citizen.

That men of Anglo-Saxon speech may have an opportunity to see and judge the Emperor from "close at hand," and view him as he appeared in the eyes of his personal attendants, these volumes have been translated, and are now submitted to the public. Though the remark of Frederick the Great that "No man is a hero to his valet" is not altogether borne out in this instance, still it will be seen that there is here nothing of that "divinity which doth hedge a king." In these volumes Napoleon appears as a man, a very great man, still a mere man, not, a demigod. Their perusal will doubtless lead to a truer conception of his character, as manifested both in his good and in his evil traits. The former were natural to him; the latter were often produced by the exceptional circumstances which surrounded him, and the extraordinary temptations to which he was subjected.

Certainly a truer and fuller light is cast by these volumes, upon the colossal figure which will always remain one of the most interesting studies in all human history.

THE TRANSLATOR.

INTRODUCTION

By Constant.

The career of a man compelled to make his own way, who is not an artisan or in some trade, does not usually begin till he is about twenty years of age. Till then he vegetates, uncertain of his future, neither having, nor being able to have, any well-defined purpose. It is only when he has arrived at the full development of his powers, and his character and bent of mind are shown, that he can determine his profession or calling. Not till then does he know himself, and see his way open before him. In fact, it is only then that he begins to live.

Reasoning in this manner, my life from my twentieth year has been thirty years, which can be divided into equal parts, so far as days and months are counted, but very unequal parts, considering the events which transpired in each of those two periods of my life.

Attached to the person of the Emperor Napoleon for fifteen years, I have seen all the men, and witnessed all the important events, which centered around him. I have seen far more than that; for I have had under my eyes all the circumstances of his life, the least as well as the greatest, the most secret as well as those which are known to history,—I have had, I repeat, incessantly under my eyes the man whose name, solitary and alone, fills the most glorious pages of our history. Fifteen years I followed him in his travels and his campaigns, was at his court, and saw him in the privacy of his family. Whatever step he wished to take, whatever order he gave, it was necessarily very difficult for the Emperor not to admit me, even though involuntarily, into his confidence; so that without desiring it, I have more than once found myself in the possession of secrets I should have preferred not to know. What wonderful things happened during those fifteen years! Those near the Emperor lived as if in the center of a whirlwind; and so quick was the succession of overwhelming events, that one felt dazed, as it were, and if he wished to pause and fix his attention for a moment, there instantly came, like another flood, a succession of events which carried him along with them without giving him time to fix his thoughts.

Succeeding these times of activity which made one's brain whirl, there came to me the most absolute repose in an isolated retreat where I passed another interval of fifteen years after leaving the Emperor. But what a contrast! To those who have lived, like myself, amid the conquests and wonders of the Empire, what is left to-day? If the strength of our manhood was passed amid the bustle of years so short, yet so fully occupied, our careers were sufficiently long and fruitful, and it is time to give ourselves up to repose. We can withdraw from the world, and close our eyes. Can it be possible to see anything equal to what we have seen? Such scenes do not come twice in the lifetime of any man; and having seen them, they suffice to occupy his memory through all his remaining years, and in retirement he can find nothing better to occupy his leisure moments than the recollections of what he has witnessed.

Thus it has been with me. The reader will readily believe that I have had no greater pleasure than that of recalling the memories of the years passed in the service of the Emperor. As far as possible, I have kept myself informed as to everything that has been written of my former master, his family, and his court; and while listening to these narrations read by my wife and sister at our fireside, the long evenings have passed like an instant! When I found in these books, some of which are truly only miserable rhapsodies, statements which were incorrect, false, or slanderous, I, took pleasure in correcting such statements, or in showing their absurdity. My wife, who lived, as I did, in the midst of these events, also made her corrections, and, without other object than our own satisfaction, made notes of our joint observations.

All who came to see us in our retreat, and took pleasure in having me narrate what I had seen, were astonished and often indignant at the falsehoods with which ignorance or malevolence had calumniated the Emperor and the Empire, and expressing their gratitude for the correct information I was able to give them, advised me also to furnish it to the public. But I attached no importance to the suggestion, and was far from dreaming that some day I should be the author of a book, until M. Ladvocat came to our hermitage, and urged me earnestly to publish my memoirs, offering himself to become the publisher.

At the very time my wife and I received this unexpected visit, we were reading together the Memoirs of Bourrienne, which the Ladvocat publishing-house had just issued; and we had remarked more than once how exempt these Memoirs were from both that spirit of disparagement and of adulation which we had noticed with disgust in other books on the same subject. M. Ladvocat advised me to complete the sketch of the

Emperor, which, owing to his elevated position and habitual occupations, Bourrienne had been able to make only from a political point of view; and in accordance with his advice, I shall relate in simple words, and in a manner suited to my relations with the Emperor, those things which Bourrienne has necessarily omitted, and which no one could know so well as I.

I candidly admit that my objections to M. Ladvocat's advice were entirely overcome when he called my attention to this passage in the introduction to Bourrienne's memoirs: "If every one who had any relations with Napoleon, whatever the time and place, will accurately and without prejudice record what he saw and heard, the future historian of his life will be rich in materials. I hope that whoever undertakes that difficult task will find in my notes some information which may be useful in perfecting his work."

Having re-read these lines attentively, I said to myself that I could furnish memoranda and information which would refute errors, brand falsehoods, and bring to light what I knew to be the truth. In a word, I felt that I could give in my testimony, and that it was my duty to do so, in the long trial which has been held ever since the overthrow of the Emperor; for I had been an eye-witness, had seen everything, and could say, "I was there." Others also have been close to the Emperor and his court, and I may often repeat what they have said, for the feats which they describe I had the same opportunity of witnessing; but, on the other hand, whatever I know of private matters, and whatever I may reveal which was secret and unknown, no one till this time could possibly have known, or consequently have related.

From the departure of the First Consul for the campaign of Marengo, whither I went with him, until the departure from Fontainebleau, when I was compelled to leave him, I was absent only twice, once for three days and once for seven or eight days. Excepting these short leaves of absence, the latter of which was on account of my health, I quitted the Emperor no more than his shadow.

It has been said that no one is a hero to his valet de chambre. I beg leave to dissent from this. The Emperor, as near as I was to him, was always a hero; and it was a great advantage also to see the man as he was. At a distance you were sensible only of the prestige of his glory and his power; but on getting closer to him you enjoyed, besides, the surprising charm of his conversation, the entire simplicity of his family life, and I do not hesitate to say, the habitual kindliness of his character.

The reader, if curious to learn beforehand in what spirit these Memoirs are written, will perhaps read with interest this passage of a letter that I wrote to my publisher:

> "Bourrienne had, perhaps, reason for treating Napoleon, as a public man, with severity. But we view him from different standpoints, and I speak only of the hero in undress. He was then almost always kind, patient, and rarely unjust. He was much attached to those about him, and received with kindness and good nature the services of those whom he liked. He was a man of habit. It is as a devoted servant that I wish to speak of the Emperor, and in no wise as a critic. It is not, however, an apotheosis in several volumes that I wish to write: for I am on this point somewhat like fathers who recognize the faults of their children, and reprove them earnestly, while at the same time they are ready to make excuses for their errors."

I trust that I shall be pardoned the familiarity, or, if you will, the inappropriateness of this comparison, for the sake of the feeling which dictates it. Besides, I do not propose either to praise or blame, but simply to relate that which fell within my knowledge, without trying to prejudice the opinion of any one.

I cannot close this introduction without a few words as to myself, in reply to the calumnies which have not spared, even in his retirement, a man who should have no enemies, if, to be protected from malice, it were sufficient to have done a little good, and no harm to any one. I am reproached with having abandoned my master after his fall, and not having shared his exile. I will show that, if I did not follow the Emperor, it was because I lacked not the will but the power to do so. God knows that I do not wish to undervalue the devotion of the faithful servants who followed the fortunes of the Emperor to the end. However, it is not improper to say that, however terrible the fall of the Emperor was for him, the situation (I speak here only of the personal advantages), in the island of Elba, of those who remained in his service, and who were not detained in France by an inexorable necessity, was still not without its advantages; and it was not, therefore, my personal interests which caused me to leave him. I shall explain hereafter my reasons for quitting his service.

I shall also give the truth as to the alleged abuse of confidence, of which, according to others, I was guilty in respect to the Emperor. A simple statement of the mistake which gave rise to this falsehood, I trust, will clear me of every suspicion of indelicacy; but if it is necessary to add other proofs, I could obtain them from those who lived nearest to the Emperor, and who were in a condition to both know and understand what passed between us; and lastly, I invoke fifty years of a blameless life, and I can say: "When I was in a situation to render great services, I did so; but I never sold them. I could have derived advantages from the petitions that I made for people, who, in consequence of my solicitations, have acquired immense fortunes; but I refused even the proper acknowledgment which in, their gratitude (very deep at that time) they felt compelled to offer me, by proposing an interest in their enterprises. I did not seek to take advantage, for my own benefit, of the generosity with which the Emperor so long deigned to honor me, in order to enrich or secure places for my relatives; and I retired poor after fifteen years passed in the personal service of the richest and most powerful monarch of Europe."

Having made these statements, I shall await with confidence the judgment of my readers.

CHAPTER I

I shall refer to myself very little in these memoirs, for I am aware the public will examine them only for details concerning the great man to whom fortune attached me for sixteen years, and whom I scarcely quitted during the whole of that time. Notwithstanding, I ask permission to say a few words as to my childhood, and the circumstances which made me valet de chambre of the Emperor.

I was born Dec. 2, 1778, at Peruelz, a town which became French on the annexation of Belgium to the Republic, and which then belonged to the Department of Jemmapes. Soon after my birth at the baths of Saint Amand, my father took charge of a small establishment called the Little Chateau, at which visitors to the waters were boarding, being aided in this enterprise by the Prince de Croi, in whose house he had been steward. Business prospered beyond my father's hopes, for a great number of invalids of rank came to his house. When I attained my eleventh year, the Count de Lure, head of one of the chief families of Valenciennes, happened to be one of the boarders at the Little Chateau; and as that excellent man had taken a great fancy to me, he asked my parents permission that I should become a companion to his son, who was about. the same age. My family had intended me for the church, to gratify one of my uncles, who was Dean of Lessine, a man of great wisdom and rigid virtue; and thinking that the offer of the Count de Lure would not affect my intended destination, my father accepted it, judging that some years passed in a family so distinguished would give me a taste for the more serious studies necessary to fit me for the priesthood. I set out, therefore, with the Count de Lure, much grieved at leaving my parents, but pleased also at the same time, as is usual with one at my age, with new scenes. The count took me to one of his estates near Tours, where I was received with the greatest kindness by the countess and her children, with whom I was placed on a footing of perfect equality.

Unfortunately I did not profit very long by the kindness of the count and the lessons. I was taught at his house, for hardly a year had passed at the chateau when we learned of the arrest of the king at Varennes. The count and his family were in despair; and child as I was, I remember that I was deeply pained at the news, without knowing why, but doubtless because it is natural to share the sentiments of those with whom you live, when they treat you with as much kindness as the count and countess had treated me. However, I continued to enjoy the happy freedom from care natural to youth, till one morning I was awakened by a loud noise, and was immediately surrounded by a great number of people, none of whom I knew, and who asked me countless questions which I could not answer. I then learned that the count and his family had emigrated. I was carried to the town hall, where the same questions were renewed, with the same fruitless result; for I knew nothing of the intentions of my late protectors, and could only reply by a flood of tears when I saw myself abandoned and left to my own resources, at a great distance from my family.

I was too young then to reflect on the conduct of the count; but I have since thought that his abandonment of me was an act of delicacy on his part, as he did not wish to make me an emigre without the consent of my parents. I have always believed that, before his departure, the count had committed me to the care of some one, who subsequently did not dare to claim me, lest he should compromise himself, which was then, as is well known, exceedingly dangerous. Behold me, then, at twelve years of age, left without a guide, without means of support, without any one to advise me, and without money, more than a hundred leagues from my home, and already accustomed to the comforts of a luxurious life. It is hardly credible that in this state of affairs I was regarded almost as a suspect, and was required each day to present myself before the city authorities for the greater safety of the Republic. I remember well that whenever the Emperor was pleased to make me relate these tribulations of my childhood, he never failed to repeat several times, "the fools," referring to these same city authorities. However that may be, the authorities of Tours, coming to the conclusion, at last, that a child of twelve was incapable of overthrowing the Republic, gave me a passport, with the injunction to leave the city within twenty-four hours, which I proceeded to do with a hearty good-will, but not without deep grief also at seeing myself alone, and on foot, with a long journey before me. After much privation and many hardships I arrived at last in the neighborhood of Saint-Amand, which I found in the possession of the Austrians, and that it was impossible for me to reach the town, as the French surrounded it. In my despair I seated myself on the side of a ditch and was weeping bitterly, when I was noticed by the chief of squadron, Michau,

> [I afterwards had the happiness of obtaining for him, from the Emperor, a position he wished, as a place of retirement, having lost the use of his right arm.—CONSTANT.]

who afterwards became colonel and aide-de-camp to General Loison. Michau approached me, questioned me with great interest, and made me relate my sad adventures, which touched him deeply, while he did not conceal his inability to send me back to my family. He had just obtained leave of absence, which he was going to spend with his family at Chinon, and proposed to me to accompany him, which invitation I accepted with gratitude. I cannot say too much of the kindness and consideration shown me by his household during the three or four months I spent with them. At the end of that time he took me to Paris, where I was soon after placed in the house of M. Gobert, a rich merchant, who treated me with the greatest, kindness.

I lately visited M. Gobert; and he recalled to me that, when we traveled together, he gave up to me one of the seats of his carriage, upon which I was permitted to stretch myself out and sleep. I mention this circumstance, otherwise unimportant, to show the kindness he always showed me.

Some years later I made the acquaintance of Carrat, who was in the service of Madame Bonaparte while the general was absent on the Egyptian expedition. Before relating how I came to enter her household, it is proper to mention how Carrat himself came into her service, and at the same time narrate some anecdotes in regard to him, which will show what were the pastimes of the inhabitants of Malmaison at that date.

Carrat happened to be at Plombieres when Madame Bonaparte

> [Madame Bonaparte, nee Marie Joseph Rose Tascher de la Pagerie, was born in Martinique, 1763; became the widow of Viscount Alexander de Beauharnais, 1794; married Napoleon Bonaparte March, 1796; became Empress May 18, 1804; was divorced Dec. 16, 1809; died at Malmaison, May 20, 1814.—TRANS.]

went there to take the waters. Every day he brought her bouquets, and addressed to her little complimentary speeches, so singular and so droll, that Josephine was much diverted, as were also the ladies who accompanied her, among whom were Mesdames de Cambis and de Criguy, and especially her own daughter Hortense, who was convulsed at his oddities. The truth is, he was exceedingly amusing, by reason of a certain simplicity and originality of character, which, however, did not prevent him from being a person of intelligence; and his eccentricities did not displease Madame Bonaparte. A sentimental scene took place when this excellent lady left the springs. Carrat wept, bemoaned himself, and expressed his lasting grief at not being able to see Madame Bonaparte daily, as he had been accustomed; and Madame Bonaparte was so kind-hearted that she at once decided to carry him to Paris with her. She taught him to dress hair, and finally appointed him her hair-dresser and valet, at least such were the duties he had to perform when I made his acquaintance.

He was permitted a most astonishing freedom of speech, sometimes even scolding her; and when Madame Bonaparte, who was extremely generous and always gracious towards every one, made presents to her women, or chatted familiarly with them, Carrat would reproach her. "Why give that?" he would say, adding, "See how you do, Madame; you allow yourself to jest with your domestics. Some day they will show you a want of respect." But if he thus endeavored to restrain the generosity of his mistress towards those around her, he did not hesitate to stimulate her generosity towards himself; and whenever he took a fancy to anything, would simply say, "You ought to give me that."

Bravery is not always the inseparable companion of wit, and Carrat gave more than once proof of this. Being endowed with a kind of simple and uncontrollable poltroonery, which never fails in comedies to excite the laughter of the spectators, it was a great pleasure to Madame Bonaparte to play on him such pranks as would bring out his singular want of courage.

It should be stated, first of all, that one of the greatest pleasures of Madame Bonaparte, at Malmaison, was to take walks on the road just outside the walls of the park; and she always preferred this outside road, in spite of the clouds of dust which were constantly rising there, to the delightful walks inside the park. One day, accompanied by her daughter Hortense, she told Carrat to follow her in her walk; and he was delighted to be thus honored until he saw rise suddenly out of a ditch; a great figure covered with a white sheet, in fact, a genuine ghost, such as I have seen described in the translations of some old English romances.

It is unnecessary to say, that the ghost was some one placed there by order of these ladies, in order to frighten Carrat; and certainly the comedy succeeded marvelously well, for as soon as Carrat perceived the ghost, he was very much frightened, and clutching Madame Bonaparte, said to her in a tremor, "Madame, Madame, do you see that ghost? It is the spirit of the lady who died lately at Plombieres."—"Be quiet, Carrat, you are a coward."—"Ah, but indeed it is her spirit which has come back." As Carrat thus spoke, the man in the white sheet advanced toward him, shaking it; and poor Carrat, overcome with terror, fell backwards in a faint, and it required all the attentions which were bestowed upon him to restore him to consciousness.

Another day, while the general was still in Egypt, and consequently before I was in the service of any member of his family, Madame Bonaparte wished to give some of her ladies an exhibition of Carrat's cowardice; and for this purpose there was concerted among the ladies of Malmaison a plot, in which Mademoiselle Hortense

[Hortense Beauharnais, born at Paris, 1783, was then just sixteen years of age. Married Louis Bonaparte and became Queen of Holland, 1806. Died 1837. She was the mother of Napoleon III. —TRANS.]

was chief conspirator. This incident has been so often narrated in my presence by Madame Bonaparte, that I am familiar with the ludicrous details. Carrat slept in a room adjoining which there was a closet. A hole was made in the wall between these rooms, and a string passed through, at the end of which was tied a can filled with water, this cooling element being suspended exactly over the head of the patient's bed. This was not all, for they had also taken the precaution to remove the slats which supported the mattress; and as Carrat was in the habit of going to sleep without a light, he saw neither the preparations for his downfall, nor the can of water provided for his new baptism. All the members of the plot had been waiting for some moments in the adjoining closet; when he threw himself heavily upon his bed, it crashed in, and at the same instant the play of the string made the can of water do its effective work. The victim at the same time of a fall, and of a nocturnal shower-bath, Carrat cried out against his double misfortune. "This is horrible," he yelled at the top of his voice; while Hortense maliciously said aloud to her mother, Madame de Crigny (afterwards Madame Denon), Madame Charvet, and to several others in the room, "Oh, Mamma, those toads and frogs in the water will get on him." These words, joined to the utter darkness, served only to increase the terror of Carrat, who, becoming seriously frightened, cried out, "It is horrible, Madame, it is horrible, to amuse yourself thus at the expense of your servants."

I do not say that the complaints of Carrat were entirely wrong, but they. served only to increase the gayety of the ladies who had taken him for the object of their pleasantries.

However that may be, such was the character and position of Carrat, whom I had known for some time, when General Bonaparte returned from his expedition into Egypt, and Carrat said to me that Eugene de Beauharnais had applied to him for a confidential valet, his own having been detained in Cairo by severe illness at the time of his departure. He was named Lefebvre, and was an old servant entirely devoted to his master, as was every one who knew Prince Eugene; for I do not believe that there has ever lived a better man, or one more polite, more considerate, or indeed more attentive, to those who served him

Carrat having told me that Eugene de Beauharnais

[Born 1781, viceroy of Italy 1805. In 1806 married the daughter of the King of Bavaria. Died 1824. Among his descendants are the present King of Sweden and the late Emperor of Brazil.—TRANS.]

desired a young man to replace Lefebvre, and having recommended me for the place, I had the good fortune to be presented to Eugene, and to give satisfaction; indeed, he was so kind as to say to me that my appearance pleased him, and he wished me to enter upon my duties immediately. I was delighted with this situation, which, I know not why, painted itself to my imagination in the brightest colors, and without loss of time, went to find my modest baggage, and behold me valet de chambre, ad interim, of M. de Beauharnais, not dreaming that I should one day be admitted to the personal service of General Bonaparte, and still less that I should become the chief valet of an Emperor.

CHAPTER II

It was on Oct. 16, 1799, that Eugene de Beauharnais arrived in Paris on his return from Egypt; and almost immediately thereafter I had the good fortune to be taken into his service, M. Eugene being then twenty-one years of age. I soon after learned a few particulars, which I think are little known, relative to his former life, and the marriage of his mother with General Bonaparte.

His father, as is well known, was one of the victims of the Revolution; and when the Marquis de Beauharnais had perished on the scaffold, his widow, whose property had been confiscated, fearing that her son, although still very young, might also be in danger on account of his belonging to the nobility, placed him in the home of a carpenter on the rue de l'Echelle where, a lady of my acquaintance, who lived on that street, has often seen him passing, carrying a plank on his shoulder. It seems a long distance from this position to the colonelcy of a regiment of the Consular guards, and the vice-royalty of Italy.

I learned, from hearing Eugene himself relate it, by what a singular circumstance he had been the cause of the first meeting between his mother and his step-father. Eugene, being then not more than fourteen or fifteen years of age, having been informed that General Bonaparte had become possessor of the sword of the Marquis de Beauharnais, took a step which seemed hazardous, but was crowned with success. The general having received him graciously, Eugene explained that he came to beg of him the restoration of his father's sword. His face, his bearing, his frank request, all made such a pleasant impression on Bonaparte, that he immediately presented him with the sword which he requested. As soon as this sword was in his hands he covered it with kisses and tears; and the whole was done in so artless a manner, that Bonaparte was delighted with him.

Madame de Beauharnais, being informed of the welcome the general had given her son, thought it her duty to make him a visit of gratitude. Bonaparte, being much pleased with Josephine in this first interview, returned her visit. They met again frequently; and as is well known, one event led to another, until she became the first Empress of the French; and I can assert from the numerous proofs that I have had of this fact, that

Bonaparte never ceased to love Eugene as well as if he, had been his own son.

The qualities of Eugene were both attractive and solid. His features were not regular, and yet his countenance prepossessed every one in his favor. He had a well-proportioned figure, but did not make a distinguished appearance, on account of the habit he had of swinging himself as he walked. He was about five feet three or four inches [About five feet six or seven inches in English measurement.—TRANS.] in height. He was kind, gay, amiable, full of wit, intelligent, generous; and it might well be said that his frank and open countenance was the mirror of his soul. How many services he has rendered others during the course of his life, and at the very period when in order to do so he had often to impose privations on himself.

It will soon be seen how it happened that I passed only a month with Eugene; but during this short space of time, I recall that, while fulfilling scrupulously his duties to his mother and his step-father, he was much addicted to the pleasures so natural to his age and position. One of his greatest pleasures was entertaining his friends at breakfast; which he did very often. This amused me much on account of the comical scenes of which I was often a witness. Besides the young officers of Bonaparte's staff, his most frequent guests, he had also frequently at his table the ventriloquist Thiemet, Dugazon, Dazincourt, and Michau of the Theatre Francais, and a few other persons, whose names escape me at this moment. As may be imagined, these reunions were extremely gay; these young officers especially, who had returned like Eugene from the expedition to Egypt, seemed trying to indemnify themselves for the recent privations they had had to suffer. At this time ventriloquists, among whom Thiemet held a very distinguished position, were the fashion in Paris, and were invited to private gatherings. I remember on one occasion, at one of these breakfasts of Eugene's, Thiemet called by their names several persons present, imitating the voices of their servants, as if they were just outside the door, while he remained quietly in his seat, appearing to be using his lips only to eat and drink, two duties' which he performed admirably. Each of the officers called in this manner went out, and found no one; and then Thiemet went out with them, under the pretext of assisting them in the search, and increased their perplexity by continuing to make them hear some well-known voice. Most of them laughed heartily at the joke of which they had just been the victims; but there was one who, having himself less under control than his comrades, took the thing seriously, and became very angry, whereupon Eugene had to avow that he was the author of the conspiracy.

I recall still another amusing scene, the two heroes of which were this same Thiemet, of whom I have just spoken, and Dugazon. Several foreigners were present at a breakfast given by Eugene, the parts having been assigned, and learned in advance, and the two victims selected. When each had taken his place at table, Dugazon, pretending to stammer, addressed a remark to Thiemet, who, playing the same role, replied to him, stammering likewise; then each of them pretended to believe that the other was making fun of him, and there followed a stuttering quarrel between the two parties, each one finding it more and more difficult to express himself as his anger rose. Thiemet, who besides his role of stammering was also playing that of deafness, addressed his neighbor, his trumpet in his ear:

"Wha-wha-what-do-does he say?"—"Nothing," replied the officious neighbor, wishing to prevent a quarrel, and to supply facts while defending the other stammerer.—"So-so-he-he-he-he's mamaking fun of me!" Then the quarrel became more violent still; they were about to come to blows, when each of the two stammerers seizing a carafe of water, hurled it at the head of his antagonist, and a copious deluge of water from the bottles taught the officious neighbors the great danger of acting as peacemakers. The two stammerers continued to scream as is the custom of deaf persons, until the last drop of water was spilt; and I remember that Eugene, the originator of this practical joke, laughed immoderately the whole time this scene lasted. The water was wiped off; and all were soon reconciled, glass in hand. Eugene, when he had perpetrated a joke of this sort, never failed to relate it to his mother, and sometimes to his stepfather, who were much amused thereby, Josephine especially.

I had led for one month a very pleasant life with Eugene, when Lefebvre, the valet de chambre whom he had left sick at Cairo, returned in restored health, and asked to resume his place. Eugene, whom I suited better on account of my age and activity, proposed to him to enter his mother's service, suggesting to him that he would there have an easier time than with himself; but Lefebvre, who was extremely attached to his master, sought Madame Bonaparte, and confided to her his chagrin at this decision.

Josephine promised to assist him; and consoled him by assurances that she would suggest to her son that Lefebvre should reassume his former position, and that she would take me into her own service. This was done according to promise; and one morning Eugene announced to me, in the most gratifying manner, my change of abode. "Constant," he said to me, "I regret very much that circumstances require us to part; but you know Lefebvre followed me to Egypt, he is an old servant, and I feel compelled to give him his former position. Besides, you will not be far removed, as you will enter my mother's service, where you will be well treated, and we will see each other often. Go to her this morning; I have spoken to her of you. The matter is already arranged, and she expects you."

As may be believed, I lost no time in presenting myself to Madame Bonaparte. Knowing that she was at Malmaison, I went there immediately, and was received by her with a kindness which overwhelmed me with gratitude, as I was not then aware that she manifested this same graciousness to every one, and that it was as inseparable from her character as was grace from her person. The duties required of me, in her service, were altogether nominal; and nearly all my time was at my own disposal, of which I took advantage to visit Paris frequently. The life that I led at this time was very pleasant to a young man like myself, who could not foresee that in a short while he would be as much under subjection as he was then at liberty.

Before bidding adieu to a service in which I had found so much that was agreeable, I will relate some incidents which belong to that period, and which my situation with the stepson of General Bonaparte gave me the opportunity of learning.

M. de Bourrienne has related circumstantially in his memoirs the events of the 18th Brumaire; [The 18th Brumaire, Nov. 9, 1799, was the day Napoleon overthrew the Directory and made himself First Consul.—TRANS.] and the account which he has given of that famous day is as correct as it is interesting, so that any one curious to know the secret causes which led to these political changes will find them faithfully pointed out in the narration of that minister of state. I am very far from intending to excite an interest of this, kind, but reading the work of M. Bourrienne put me again on the track of my own recollections. These memoirs relate to circumstances of which he was ignorant, or possibly may have omitted purposely as being of little importance; and whatever he has let fall on his road I think myself fortunate in being permitted to glean.

I was still with Eugene de Beauharnais when General Bonaparte overthrew the Directory; but I found myself in as favorable a situation to know all that was passing as if I had been in the service of Madame Bonaparte, or of the general himself, for my master, although he was very young, had the entire confidence of his stepfather, and, to an even greater degree, that of his mother, who consulted him on every occasion.

A few days before the 18th Brumaire, Eugene ordered me to make preparations for a breakfast he wished to give on that day to his friends, the number of the guests, all military men, being much larger than usual. This bachelor repast was made very gay by an officer, who amused the company by imitating in turn the manners and appearance of the directors and a few of their friends. To represent the Director Barras, he draped himself 'a la grecque' with the tablecloth, took off his black cravat, turned down his shirt-collar, and advanced in an affected manner, resting his left arm on the shoulder of the youngest of his comrades, while with his right he pretended to caress his chin. Each person of the company understood the meaning of that kind of charade; and there were uncontrollable bursts of laughter.

He undertook then to represent the Abbe Sieyes, by placing an enormous band of paper inside of his neckcloth, and lengthening thus indefinitely a long, pale face. He made a few turns around the room, astraddle of his chair, and ended by a grand somersault, as if his steed had dismounted him. It is necessary to know, in order to understand the significance of this pantomime, that the Abbe Sieges had been recently taking lessons in horseback, riding in the garden of the Luxembourg, to the great amusement of the pedestrians, who gathered in crowds to enjoy the awkward and ungraceful exhibition made by this new master of horse.

The breakfast ended, Eugene reported for duty to General Bonaparte, whose aide-de-camp he was, and his friends rejoined the various commands to which they belonged.

I went out immediately behind them; for from a few words that had just been dropped at my young master's, I suspected that something grave and interesting was about to take place. M. Eugene had appointed a rendezvous with his comrades at Pont-Tournant; so I repaired to that spot, and found a considerable gathering of officers in uniform and on horseback, assembled in readiness to escort General Bonaparte to Saint- Cloud.

The commandant of each part of the army had been requested by General Bonaparte to give a breakfast to their corps of officers; and they had done so like my young master. Nevertheless, the officers, even the generals, were not all in the secret; and General Murat himself, who rushed into the Hall of the Five Hundred at the head of the grenadiers, believed that it was only a question of exemption, on account of age, that General Bonaparte intended to propose, in order that he might obtain the place of director.

I have learned from an authoritative source, that when General Jube, who was devoted to General Bonaparte, assembled in the court of the Luxembourg, the guard of the directors of which he was commander, the honest M. Gohier, president of the Directory, put his head out of the window, and cried to Jube: "Citizen General, what are you doing down there?"—"Citizen President, you can see for yourself I am mustering the guard."—"Certainly, I see that very plainly, Citizen General; but why are you mustering them?"—"Citizen President, I am going to make an inspection of them, and order a grand maneuver. Forward—march!" And the citizen general filed out at the head of his troop to rejoin General Bonaparte at Saint-Cloud; while the latter was awaited at the house of the citizen president, and the breakfast delayed to which General Bonaparte had been invited for that very morning.

General Marmont had also entertained at breakfast the officers of the division of the army which he commanded (it was, I think, the artillery). At the end of the repast he addressed a few words to them, urging them not to alienate their cause from that of the conqueror of Italy, and to accompany him to Saint-Cloud. "But how can we follow him?" cried one of his guests. "We have no horses."—"If that alone deters you, you will find horses in the court of this hotel. I have seized all those of the national riding-school. Let us go below and mount." All the officers present responded to the invitation except General Allix, who declared he would take no part in all this disturbance.

I was at Saint-Cloud on the two days, 18th and 19th Brumaire. I saw General Bonaparte harangue the soldiers, and read to them the decree by which he had been made commander-in-chief of all the troops at Paris, and of the whole of the Seventeenth Military Division. I saw him come out much agitated first from the Council of the Ancients, and afterwards from the Assembly of the Five Hundred. I saw Lucien Bonaparte brought out of the hall, where the latter assembly was sitting, by some grenadiers, sent in to protect him from the violence of his colleagues. Pale and furious, he threw himself on his horse and galloped straight to the troops to address them; and when he pointed his sword at his brother's breast, saying he would be the first to slay him if he dared to strike at liberty, cries of "Vive Bonaparte! down with the lawyers!" burst forth on all sides; and the soldiers, led by General Murat, rushed into the Hall of the Five Hundred. Everybody knows what then occurred, and I will not enter into details which have been so often related.

The general, now made First Consul, installed himself at the Luxembourg, though at this time he resided also at Malmaison. But he was often on the road, as was also Josephine; for their trips to Paris when they occupied this residence were very frequent, not only on Government business, which often required the presence of the First Consul, but also for the purpose of attending the theater, of whose performances General Bonaparte, was very fond, giving the preference always to the Theatre Francais and the Italian Opera. This observation I make in passing, preferring to give hereafter the information I have obtained as to the tastes and habits of the emperor.

Malmaison, at the period of which I speak, was a place of unalloyed happiness, where all who came expressed their satisfaction with the state of affairs; everywhere also I heard blessings invoked upon the First Consul and Madame Bonaparte. There was not yet the shadow of that strict etiquette which it was necessary afterwards to observe at Saint-Cloud, at the Tuileries, and in all the palaces in which the Emperor held his court. The consular court was as yet distinguished by a simple elegance, equally removed from republican rudeness and the luxuriousness of the Empire. Talleyrand was, at this period, one of those who came most frequently to

Malmaison. He sometimes dined there, but arrived generally in the evening between eight and nine o'clock, and returned at one, two, and sometimes three in the morning.

All were admitted at Madame Bonaparte's on a footing of equality, which was most gratifying. There came familiarly Murat, Duroc, Berthier, and all those who have since figured as great dignitaries, and some even as sovereigns, in the annals of the empire.

The family of General Bonaparte were assiduous in their attentions; but it was known among us that they had no love for Madame Bonaparte, of which fact I had many proofs. Mademoiselle Hortense never left her mother, and they were devotedly attached to each other.

Besides men distinguished by their posts under the government or in the army, there gathered others also who were not less distinguished by personal merit, or the position which their birth had given them before the Revolution. It was a veritable panorama, in which we saw the persons themselves pass before our eyes. The scene itself, even exclusive of the gayety which always attended the dinings of Eugene, had its attractions. Among those whom we saw most frequently were Volney, Denon, Lemercier, the Prince of Poix, de Laigle, Charles Baudin, General Beurnonville, Isabey, and a number of others, celebrated in science, literature, and art; in short, the greater part of those who composed the society of Madame de Montesson.

Madame Bonaparte and Mademoiselle Hortense often took excursions on horseback into the country. On these occasions her most constant escorts were the Prince de Poix and M. de Laigle. One day, as this party was reentering the court-yard at Malmaison, the horse which Hortense rode became frightened, and dashed off. She was an accomplished rider, and very active, so she attempted to spring off on the grass by the roadside; but the band which fastened the end of her riding-skirt under her foot prevented her freeing herself quickly, and she was thrown, and dragged by her horse for several yards. Fortunately the gentlemen of the party, seeing her fall, sprang from their horses in time to rescue her; and, by extraordinary good fortune, she was not even bruised, and was the first to laugh at her misadventure.

During the first part of my stay at Malmaison, the First Consul always slept with his wife, like an ordinary citizen of the middle classes in Paris; and I heard no rumor of any intrigue in the chateau. The persons of this society, most of whom were young, and who were often very numerous, frequently took part in sports which recalled college days. In fact, one of the greatest diversions of the inhabitants of Malmaison was to play "prisoners' base." It was usually after dinner; and Bonaparte, Lauriston, Didelot, de Lucay, de Bourrienne, Eugene, Rapp, Isabey, Madame Bonaparte, and Mademoiselle

Hortense would divide themselves into two camps, in which the prisoners taken, or exchanged, would recall to the First Consul the greater game, which he so much preferred. In these games the most active runners were Eugene, Isabey, and Hortense. As to General Bonaparte, he often fell, but rose laughing boisterously.

General Bonaparte and his family seemed to enjoy almost unexampled happiness, especially when at Malmaison, which residence, though agreeable at that time, was far from being what it has since become. This estate consisted of the chateau, which Bonaparte found in bad condition on his return from Egypt, a park already somewhat improved, and a farm, the income of which did not with any certainty exceed twelve thousand francs a year. Josephine directed in person all the improvements made there, and no woman ever possessed better taste.

From the first, they played amateur comedy at Malmaison, which was a relaxation the First Consul enjoyed greatly, but in which he took no part himself except that of looker-on. Every one in the house attended these representations; and I must confess we felt perhaps even more pleasure than others in seeing thus travestied on the stage those in whose service we were.

The Malmaison Troupe, if I may thus style actors of such exalted social rank, consisted principally of Eugene, Jerome, Lauriston, de Bourrienne, Isabey, de Leroy, Didelot, Mademoiselle Hortense, Madame Caroline Murat, and the two Mademoiselles Auguie, one of whom afterwards married Marshal Ney,

> [Michel Ney, Styled by Napoleon the "bravest of the brave," was born 1769, at Sarre-Louis (now in Prussia), son of a cooper. Entered the army as a private 1787, adjutant-general 1794, general of brigade 1796, general of division 1799, marshal 1804, Duke of Elchingen 1805, Prince of Moskwa 1812, and commanded the rear-guard in the famous retreat from Russia. On the return from Elba he went over to Napoleon; was at Waterloo. Was afterwards taken, and in spite of the terms of the surrender of Paris was tried for treason, and shot in the gardens of the Luxembourg, Dec. 8, 1815.—TRANS.]

and the other M. de Broc. All four were very young and charming, and few theaters in Paris could show four actresses as pretty. In addition to which, they showed much grace in their acting, and played their parts with real talent; and were as natural on the stage as in the saloon, where they bore themselves with exquisite grace and refinement. At first the repertoire contained little variety, though the pieces were generally well selected. The first representation which I attended was the "Barber of Seville "in which Isabey played the role of Figaro, and Mademoiselle Hortense that of Rosine—and the "Spiteful Lover." Another time I saw played the "Unexpected Wager," and "False Consultations." Hortense and Eugene played this last piece perfectly; and I still recall that, in the role of Madame le Blanc, Hortense appeared prettier than ever in the character of an old woman, Eugene representing Le Noir, and Lauriston the charlatan. The First Consul, as I have said, confined himself to the role of spectator; but he seemed to take in these fireside plays, so to speak, the greatest pleasure, laughed and applauded heartily, though sometimes he also criticised.

Madame Bonaparte was also highly entertained; and even if she could not always boast of the successful acting of her children, "the chiefs of the troupe," it sufficed her that it was an agreeable relaxation to her husband, and seemed to give him pleasure; for her constant study was to contribute to the happiness of the great man who had united her destiny with his own.

When the day for the presentation of a play had been appointed, there was never any postponement, but often a change of the play; not because of the indisposition, or fit of the blues, of an actress (as often happens in the theaters of Paris), but for more serious reasons. It sometimes happened that M. d'Etieulette received orders to rejoin his regiment, or an important mission was confided to Count Almaviva, though Figaro and Rosine always remained at their posts; and the desire of pleasing the First Consul was, besides, so general among all those who surrounded him, that the substitutes did their best in the absence of the principals, and the play never failed for want of an actor.

> [Michau, of the Comedie Francaise, was the instructor of the troupe. Wherever it happened that an actor was wanting in animation, Michau would exclaim. "Warmth! Warmth! Warmth! Warmth!" —Note by CONSTANT.]

CHAPTER III

I had been only a very short time in the service of Madame Bonaparte when I made the acquaintance of Charvet, the concierge of Malmaison, and in connection with this estimable man became each day more and more intimate, till at last he gave me one of his daughters in marriage. I was eager to learn from him all that he could tell me concerning Madame Bonaparte and the First Consul prior to my entrance into the house; and in our frequent conversations he took the greatest pleasure in satisfying my curiosity. It is to him I owe the following details as to the mother and daughter.

When General Bonaparte set out for Egypt, Madame Bonaparte accompanied him as far as Toulon, and was extremely anxious to go with him to Egypt. When the general made objections, she observed that having been born a Creole, the heat of the climate would be more favorable than dangerous to her. By a singular coincidence it was on 'La Pomone' that she wished to make the journey; that is to say, on the very same vessel which in her early youth had brought her from Martinique to France. General Bonaparte, finally yielding to the wishes of his wife, promised to send 'La Pomone' for her, and bade her go in the meantime to take the waters at Plombieres. The matter being arranged between husband and wife, Madame Bonaparte was delighted to go to the springs of Plombieres which she had desired to visit for a long time, knowing, like every one else, the reputation these waters enjoyed for curing barrenness in women.

Madame Bonaparte had been only a short time at Plombieres, when one morning, while occupied in hemming a turban and chatting with the ladies present, Madame de Cambis, who was on the balcony, called to her to come and see a pretty little dog passing along the street. All the company hastened with Madame Bonaparte to the balcony, which caused it to fall with a frightful crash. By a most fortunate chance, no one was killed; though Madame de Cambis had her leg broken, and Madame Bonaparte was most painfully bruised, without, however, receiving any fracture. Charvet, who was in a room behind the saloon, heard the noise, and at once had a sheep killed and skinned, and Madame Bonaparte wrapped in the skin. It was a long while before she regained her health, her arms and her hands especially being so bruised that she was for a long time unable to use them; and it was necessary to cut up her food, feed her, and, in fact, perform the same offices for her as for an infant.

I related above that Josephine thought she was to rejoin her husband in Egypt, and consequently that her stay at the springs of Plombieres would be of short duration but her accident led her to think that it would be prolonged indefinitely; she therefore desired, while waiting for her complete recovery, to have with her her daughter Hortense, then about fifteen years of age, who was being educated in the boarding-school of Madame Campan. She sent for her a mulatto woman to whom she was much attached, named Euphemie, who was the foster-sister of Madame Bonaparte, and passed (I do not know if the supposition was correct) as her natural sister. Euphemie, accompanied by Charvet, made the journey in one of Madame Bonaparte's carriages. Mademoiselle Hortense, on their arrival, was delighted with the journey she was about to make, and above all with the idea of being near her mother, for whom she felt the tenderest affection. Mademoiselle Hortense was, I would not say, greedy, but she was exceedingly fond of sweets; and Charvet, in relating these details, said to me, that at each town of any size through which they passed the carriage was filled with bonbons and dainties, of which mademoiselle consumed a great quantity. One day, while Euphemie and Charvet were sound asleep, they were suddenly awakened by a report, which sounded frightful to them, and caused them intense anxiety, as they found when they awoke that they were passing through a thick forest. This ludicrous incident threw Hortense into fits of laughter; for hardly had they expressed their alarm when they found themselves deluged with an odoriferous froth, which explained the cause of the explosion. A bottle of champagne, placed in one of the pockets of the carriage, had been uncorked; and the heat, added to the motion of the carriage, or rather the malice of the young traveler, had made it explode with a loud report.

When mademoiselle arrived at Plombieres, her mother's health was almost restored; so that the pupil of Madame Campan found there all the distractions which please and delight at the age which the daughter of Madame Bonaparte had then attained.

There is truth in the saying that in all evil there is good, for had this accident not happened to Madame Bonaparte, it is very probable she would have become a prisoner of the English; in fact, she learned that 'La Pomone', the vessel on which she wished to make the voyage, had fallen into the power of the enemies of France. General Bonaparte, in all his letters, still dissuaded his wife from the plan she had of rejoining him; and, consequently, she returned to Paris.

On her arrival Josephine devoted her attention to executing a wish General Bonaparte had expressed to her before leaving. He had remarked to her that he should like, on his return, to have a country seat; and he charged his brother to attend to this, which Joseph, however, failed to do. Madame Bonaparte, who, on the contrary, was always in search of what might please her husband, charged several persons to make excursions in the environs of Paris, in order to ascertain whether a suitable dwelling could be found. After having vacillated long between Ris and Malmaison, she decided on the latter, which she bought from M. Lecoulteux-Dumoley, for, I think, four hundred thousand francs. Such were the particulars which Charvet was kind enough to give me when I first entered the service of Madame Bonaparte. Every one in the house loved to speak of her; and it was certainly not to speak evil, for never was woman more beloved by all who surrounded her, and never has one deserved it more. General Bonaparte was also an excellent man in the retirement of private life.

After the return of the First Consul from his campaign in Egypt, several attempts against his life had been made; and the police had warned him many times to be on his guard, and not to risk himself alone in the environs of Malmaison. The First Consul had been very careless up to this period; but the discovery of the snares which were laid for him, even in the privacy of his family circle, forced him to use precautions and prudence. It has been stated since, that these pretended plots were only fabrications of the police to render themselves necessary to the First Consul, or, perhaps, of the First Consul himself, to redouble the interest which attached to his person, through fear of the perils which menaced his life; and the absurdity of these attempts is alleged as proof of this. I could not pretend to elucidate such mysteries; but it seems to me that in such matters absurdity proves nothing, or, at least, it does not prove that such plots did not exist. The conspirators of that period set no bounds to their extravagance; for what could be more absurd, and at the same time more real, than the atrocious folly of the infernal machine?

Be that as it may, I shall relate what passed under my own eyes during the first month of my stay at Malmaison. No one there, or, at least, no one in my presence, showed the least doubt of the reality of these attempts.

In order to get rid of the First Consul, all means appeared good to his enemies: they noted everything in their calculations, even his absence of mind. The following occurrence is proof of this:

There were repairs and ornamentations to be made to the mantel in the rooms of the First Consul at Malmaison. The contractor in charge of this work had sent marblecutters, amongst whom had slipped in, it seems, a few miserable wretches employed by the conspirators. The persons attached to the First Consul were incessantly on the alert, and exercised the greatest watchfulness; and it was observed that among these workmen there were men who pretended to work, but whose air and manner contrasted strongly with their occupation. These suspicions were unfortunately only too well founded; for when the apartments had been made ready to receive the First Consul, and just as he was on the eve of occupying them, some one making a final inspection found on the desk at which he would first seat himself, a snuff-box, in every respect like one of those which he constantly used. It was thought at first that this box really belonged to him, and that it had been forgotten and left there by his valet; but doubts inspired by the suspicious manner of a few of the marble-cutters, leading to further investigation, the tobacco was examined and analyzed. It was found to be poisoned.

The authors of this perfidy had, it is said, at this time, communication with other conspirators, who engaged to attempt another means of ridding themselves of the First Consul. They promised to attack the guard of the chateau (Malmaison), and to carry off by force the chief of the government. With this intention, they had uniforms made like those of the consular guards, who then stood sentinel, day and night, over the First Consul, and followed him on horseback in his excursions. In this costume, and by the aid of signals, with their accomplices (the pretended marble-cutters) on the inside, they could easily have approached and mingled with the guard, who were fed and quartered at the chateau. They could even have reached the First Consul, and carried him off. However, this first project was abandoned as too uncertain; and the conspirators flattered themselves that they would succeed in their undertaking more surely, and with less danger, by taking advantage of the frequent journeys of the First Consul to Paris. By means of their disguise they planned to distribute themselves on the road, among the guides of the escort, and massacre them, their rallying-point being the quarries of Nanterre; but their plots were for the second time foiled. There was in the park at Malmaison a deep quarry; and fears being entertained that they would profit by it to conceal themselves therein, and exercise some violence against the First Consul on one of his solitary walks, it was decided to secure it with an iron door.

On the 19th of February, at one in the afternoon, the First Consul went in state to the Tuileries, which was then called the Government palace, to install himself there with all his household. With him were his two colleagues; one of whom, the third consul, was to occupy the same residence, and be located in the Pavilion de Flore. The carriage of the consuls was drawn by six white horses, which the Emperor of Germany had presented to the conqueror of Italy after the signature of the treaty of peace of Campo-Formio. The saber that the First Consul wore at this ceremony was magnificent, and had also been presented to him by this monarch on the same occasion.

A remarkable thing in this formal change of residence was that the acclamations and enthusiasm of the crowd, and even of the most distinguished spectators, who filled the windows of rue Thionville and of the quai Voltaire, were addressed only to the First Consul, and to the young warriors of his brilliant staff, who were yet bronzed by the sun of the Pyramids or of Italy. At their head rode General Lannes and Murat; the first easy to recognize by his bold bearing and soldierly manners; the second by the same qualities, and further by a striking elegance, both of costume and equipments. His new title of brother-in-law of the First Consul contributed, also, greatly to fix upon him the attention of all. As for myself, all my attention was absorbed by the principal personage of the cortege, whom, like every one around me, I regarded with something like a religious reverence; and by his stepson, the son of my excellent mistress, himself once my master,—the brave, modest, good Prince Eugene, who at that time, however, was not yet a prince. On his arrival at the Tuileries, the First Consul took possession at once of the apartments which he afterwards occupied, and which were formerly part of the royal apartments. These apartments consisted of a bed-chamber, a bathroom, a cabinet, and a saloon, in which he gave audience in the forenoon; of a second saloon, in which were stationed his aides-de-camp on duty, and which he used as a dining-room; and also a very large antechamber. Madame Bonaparte had her separate apartments on the ground floor, the same which she afterwards occupied as Empress. Beneath the suite of rooms occupied by the First Consul was the room of Bourrienne, his private secretary, which communicated with the apartments of the First Consul by means of a private staircase.

Although at this period there were already courtiers, there was not, however, yet a court, and the etiquette was exceedingly simple. The First Consul, as I believe I have already said, slept in the same bed with his wife; and they lived together, sometimes at the Tuileries, sometimes at Malmaison. As yet there were neither grand marshal, nor chamberlains, nor prefects of the palace, nor ladies of honor, nor lady ushers, nor ladies of the wardrobe, nor pages. The household of the First Consul was composed only of M. Pfister, steward; Venard, chief cook; Galliot, and Dauger, head servants; Colin, butler. Ripeau was librarian; Vigogne, senior, in charge of the stables. Those attached to his personal service were Hambard, head valet; Herbert, ordinary valet; and Roustan, mameluke of the First Consul. There were, beside these, fifteen persons to discharge the ordinary duties of the household. De Bourrienne superintended everything, and regulated expenses, and, although very strict, won the esteem and affection of every one.

He was kind, obliging, and above all very just; and consequently at the time of his disgrace the whole household was much distressed. As for myself, I retain a sincerely respectful recollection of him; and I believe that, though he has had the misfortune to find enemies among the great, he found among his inferiors only grateful hearts and sincere regrets.

Some days after this installation, there was at the chateau a reception of the diplomatic corps. It will be seen from the details, which I shall give, how very simple at that time was the etiquette of what they already called the Court.

At eight o'clock in the evening, the apartments of Madame Bonaparte, situated, as I have just said, on the ground floor adjoining the garden, were crowded with people. There was an incredible wealth of plumes, diamonds, and dazzling toilets. The crowd was so great that it was found necessary to throw open the bedroom of Madame Bonaparte, as the two saloons were so full there was not room to move.

When, after much embarrassment and difficulty, every one had found a place as they could, Madame Bonaparte was announced, and entered, leaning on the arm of Talleyrand. She wore a dress of white muslin with short sleeves, and a necklace of pearls. Her head was uncovered; and the beautiful braids of her hair, arranged with charming negligence, were held in place by a tortoise-shell comb. The flattering murmur which greeted her appearance was most grateful to her; and never, I believe, did she display more grace and majesty.

Talleyrand,

> [Charles Maurice de Talleyrand-Perigord, born at Paris, 1754, was descended from the counts of Perigord. Rendered lame by an accident, he entered the clergy, and in 1788 became Bishop of Autun. In the States-General he sided with the Revolution. During the Reign of Terror he visited England and the United States. Recalled in 1796, he became minister of foreign affairs under the Directory, which post he retained under the Consulate. In 1806 he was made Prince of Benevento. He soon fell into disgrace. Sided with the Bourbons in 1814, and was minister at the congress of Vienna, president of the council, and minister under the king. Died 1838. —TRANS.]

giving his hand to Madame Bonaparte, had the honor of presenting to her, one after another, the members of the Diplomatic Corps, not according to their names, but that of the courts they represented. He then made with her the tour of the two saloons, and the circuit of the second was only half finished when the First Consul entered without being announced. He was dressed in a very plain uniform, with a tricolored silk scarf, with fringes of the same around his waist. He wore close-fitting pantaloons of white cassimere, and top-boots, and held his hat in his hand. This plain dress, in the midst of the embroidered coats loaded with cordons and orders worn by the ambassadors and foreign dignitaries, presented a contrast as striking as the toilette of Madame Bonaparte compared with that of the other ladies present.

Before relating how I exchanged the service of Madame Bonaparte for that of the chief of state, and a sojourn at Malmaison for the second campaign of Italy, I think I should pause to recall one or two incidents which belong to the time spent in the service of Madame Bonaparte. She loved to sit up late, and, when almost everybody else had retired, to play a game of billiards, or more often of backgammon. It happened on one occasion that, having dismissed every one else, and not yet being sleepy, she asked if I knew how to play billiards, and upon my replying in the affirmative, requested me with charming grace to play with her; and I had often afterwards the honor of doing so. Although I had some skill, I always managed to let her beat me, which pleased her exceedingly. If this was flattery, I must admit it; but I would have done the same towards any other woman, whatever her rank and her relation to me, had she been even half as lovely as was Madame Bonaparte.

The concierge of Malmaison, who possessed the entire confidence of his employers, among other means of precaution and watchfulness conceived by him in order to protect the residence and person of the First Consul from any sudden attack, had trained for the chateau several large dogs, among which were two very handsome Newfoundlands. Work on the improvements of Malmaison went on incessantly, and a large number of workmen lodged there at night, who were carefully warned not to venture out alone; but one night as some of the watchdogs were with the workmen in their lodgings, and allowed themselves to be caressed, their apparent docility encouraged one of these men to attempt the imprudence of venturing out. Believing that the surest way to avoid danger was to put himself under the protection of one of those powerful animals, he took one of them with him, and in a very friendly manner they passed out of the door together; but no sooner had they reached the outside, than the dog sprang upon his unfortunate companion and threw him down. The cries of the poor workman brought some of the guard, who ran to his aid. Just in time; for the dog was holding him fast to the ground, and had seized him by the throat. He was rescued, badly wounded. Madame Bonaparte, when she was informed of this accident, had him nursed till perfectly cured, and gave him a handsome gratuity, but recommended him to be more prudent in the future.

Every moment that the First Consul could snatch from affairs of state he passed at Malmaison. The evening of each decadii

[Under the Republic, Sunday was abolished. A decade of ten days was substituted for the week; and the decadi, or tenth day, took the place of the Sabbath.—TRANS.]

was a time of expectation and joy at the chateau. Madame Bonaparte sent domestics on horseback and on foot to meet her husband, and often went herself, accompanied by her daughter and her Malmaison friends. When not on duty, I went myself and alone: for everybody felt for the First Consul the same affection, and experienced in regard to him the same anxiety; and such was the bitterness and boldness of his enemies that the road, though short, between Paris and Malmaison was full of dangers and snares. We knew that many plans had been laid to kidnap him on this road, and that these attempts might be renewed. The most dangerous spot was the quarries of Nanterre, of which I have already spoken; so they were carefully examined, and guarded by his followers each day on which the First Consul was to pass, and finally the depressions nearest the road were filled up. The First Consul was gratified by our devotion to him, and gave us proofs of his satisfaction, though he himself seemed always free from fear or uneasiness. Very often, indeed, he mildly ridiculed our anxiety, and would relate very seriously to the good Josephine what a narrow escape he had on the road; how men of a sinister appearance had shown themselves many times on his way; how one of them had had the boldness to aim at him, etc. And when he saw her well frightened, he would burst out laughing, give her some taps or kisses on her cheek and neck, saying to her, "Have no fear, little goose; they would not dare." On these "days of furlough," as he called them, he was occupied more with his private affairs than with those of state; but never could he remain idle. He would make them pull down, put up again, build, enlarge, set out, prune, incessantly, both in the chateau and in the park, while he examined the bills of expenses, estimated receipts, and ordered economies. Time passed quickly in all these occupations; and the moment soon came when it was necessary to return, and, as he expressed it, put on again the yoke of misery.

CHAPTER IV

Towards the end of March, 1800, five or six months after my entrance into the service of Madame. Bonaparte, the First Consul while at dinner one day regarded me intently; and having carefully scrutinized and measured me from head to foot, "Young man," said he, "would you like to go with me on the campaign?" I replied, with much emotion, that I would ask nothing better. "Very well, then, you shall go with me!" and on rising from the table, he ordered Pfister, the steward, to place my name on the list of the persons of his household who would accompany him. My preparations did not require much time; for I was delighted with the idea of being attached to the personal service of so great a man, and in imagination saw myself already beyond the Alps. But the First Consul set out without me. Pfister, by a defect of memory, perhaps intentional, had forgotten to place my name on the list. I was in despair, and went to relate, with tears, my misfortune to my excellent mistress, who was good enough to endeavor to console me, saying, "Well, Constant, everything is not lost; you will stay with me. You can hunt in the park to pass the time; and perhaps the First Consul may yet send for you." However, Madame Bonaparte did not really believe this; for she thought, as I did, although out of kindness she did not wish to say this to me, that the First Consul having changed his mind, and no longer wishing my services on the campaign, had himself given the counter orders. However, I soon had proof to the contrary. In passing through Dijon, on his way to Mt. St. Bernard, the First Consul asked for me, and learning that they had forgotten me, expressed his dissatisfaction, and directed Bourrienne to write immediately to Madame Bonaparte, requesting her to send me on without delay.

One morning, when my chagrin was more acute than ever, Madame Bonaparte sent for me, and said, holding Bourrienne's letter in her hand, "Constant, since you have determined to quit us to make the campaign, you may rejoice, for you are now about to leave. The First Consul has sent for you. Go to the office of Maret, and ascertain if he will not soon send a courier. You will accompany him." I was inexpressibly delighted at this good news, and did not try to conceal my pleasure. "You are very well satisfied to leave us," said Madame Bonaparte with a kind smile. "It is not leaving Madame, but joining the First Consul, which delights me." —"I hope so," replied she. "Go, Constant; and take good care of him." If any incentive had been needed, this injunction of my noble mistress would have added to the zeal and fidelity with which I had determined to discharge my new duties. I hurried without delay to the office of Maret, secretary of state, who already knew me, and had shown his good-will for me. "Get ready at once," said he; "a courier will set out this evening or to-morrow morning." I returned in all haste to Malmaison, and announced to Madame Bonaparte my immediate departure. She immediately had a good post-chaise made ready for me, and Thibaut (for that was the name of the courier I was to accompany) was directed to obtain horses for me along the route. Maret gave me eight hundred francs for the expenses of my trip, which sum, entirely unexpected by me, filled me with wonder, for I had never been so rich. At four o'clock in the morning, having heard from Thibaut that everything was ready, I went to his house, where the post-chaise awaited me, and we set out.

I traveled very comfortably, sometimes in the postchaise, sometimes on horseback; I taking Thibaut's place, and he mine. I expected to overtake the First Consul at Martigny; but his traveling had been so rapid, that I caught up with him only at the convent of Mt. St. Bernard. Upon our route we constantly passed regiments on the march, composed of officers and soldiers who were hastening to rejoin their different corps. Their enthusiasm was irrepressible,—those who had made the campaign of Italy rejoiced at returning to so fine a country; those who had not yet done so were burning with impatience to see the battlefields immortalized by French valor, and by the genius of the hero who still marched at their head. All went as if to a festival, and singing songs they climbed the mountains of Valais. It was eight o'clock in the morning when I arrived at headquarters. Pfister announced me; and I found the general-in-chief in the great hall, in the basement of the Hospice. He was taking breakfast, standing, with his staff. As soon as he saw me, he said, "Here you are, you queer fellow! why didn't you come with me?" I excused myself by saying that to my great regret I had received a counter order, or, at least, they had left me behind at the moment of departure. "Lose no time, my friend; eat quickly; we are about to start." From this moment I was attached to the personal service of the First Consul, in the quality of ordinary valet; that is to say, in my turn. This duty gave me little to do; Hambard, the head valet of the First Consul, being in the habit of dressing him from head to foot.

Immediately after breakfast we began to descend the mountain, many sliding down on the snow, very much as they coast at the garden

Beaujon, from top to bottom of the Montagnes Russes, and I followed their example. This they called "sledding." The general-in-chief also descended in this manner an almost perpendicular glacier. His guide was a young countryman, active and courageous, to whom the First Consul promised a sufficiency for the rest of his days. Some young soldiers who had wandered off into the snow were found, almost dead with cold, by the dogs sent out by the monks, and carried to the Hospice, where they received every possible attention, and their lives were saved. The First Consul gave substantial proof of his gratitude to the good fathers for a charity so useful and generous. Before leaving the Hospice, where he had found tables loaded with food already prepared awaiting the soldiers as soon as they reached the summit of the mountain, he gave to the good monks a considerable sum of money, in reward for the hospitality he and his companions in arms had received, and an order on the treasury for an annuity in support of the convent.

The same day we climbed Mount Albaredo; but as this passage was impracticable for cavalry and artillery, he ordered them to pass outside the town of Bard, under the batteries of the fort. The First Consul had ordered that they should pass it at night, and on a gallop; and he had straw tied around the wheels of the caissons and on the feet of the horses, but even these precautions were not altogether sufficient to prevent the Austrians hearing our troops. The cannon of the fort rained grape-shot incessantly; but fortunately the houses of the town sheltered our soldiers from the enemy's guns, and more than half the army passed without much loss. I was with the household of the First Consul, which under the care of General Gardanne flanked the fort.

The 23d of May we forded a torrent which flowed between the town and the fort, with the First Consul at our head, and then, followed by General Berthier and some other officers, took the path over the Albaredo, which overlooked the fort and the town of Bard. Directing his field-glass towards the hostile batteries, from the fire of which he was protected only by a few bushes, he criticised the dispositions which had been made by the officer in charge of the siege of the fort, and ordered changes, which he said would cause the place to fall into our hands in a short time. Freed now from the anxiety which this fort had caused him, and which he said had prevented his sleeping the two days he had passed in the convent of Maurice, he stretched himself at the foot of a fir-tree and took a refreshing nap, while the army was making good its passage. Rising from this brief interval of repose, he descended the mountain and continued his march to Ivree, where we passed the night.

The brave General Lannes, who commanded the advance guard, acted somewhat in the capacity of quartermaster, taking possession of all the places which barred the road. Only a few hours before we entered he had forced the passage of Ivree.

Such was this miraculous passage of St. Bernard. Horses, cannon, caissons, and an immense quantity of army stores of all kinds, everything, in fact, was drawn or carried over glaciers which appeared inaccessible, and by paths which seemed impracticable even for a single man. The Austrian cannon were not more successful than the snow in stopping the French army. So true is it that the genius and perseverance of the First Consul were communicated, so to speak, to the humblest of his soldiers, and inspired them with a courage and a strength, the results of which will appear fabulous to posterity.

On the 2d of June, which was the day after the passage of the Ticino, and the day of our entrance into Milan, the First Consul learned that the fort of Bard had been taken the evening before, showing that his dispositions had led to a quick result, and the road of communication by the St. Bernard was now free from all obstructions. The First Consul entered Milan without having met much resistance, the whole population turned out on his entrance, and he was received with a thousand acclamations. The confidence of the Milanese redoubled when they learned that he had promised the members of the assembled clergy to maintain the catholic worship and clergy as already established, and had compelled them to take the oath of fidelity to the cisalpine republic.

The First Consul remained several days in this capital; and I had time to form a more intimate acquaintance with my colleagues, who were, as I have said, Hambard, Roustan, and Hebert. We relieved each other every twenty- four hours, at noon precisely. As has always been my rule when thrown into association with strangers, I observed, as closely as circumstances permitted, the character and temper of my comrades, so that I could regulate my conduct in regard to them, and know in advance what I might have to fear or hope from association with them.

Hambard had an unbounded devotion for the First Consul, whom he had followed to Egypt, but unfortunately his temper was gloomy and misanthropic, which made him extremely sullen and disagreeable; and the favor which Roustan enjoyed perhaps contributed to increase this gloomy disposition. In a kind of mania he imagined himself to be the object of a special espionage; and when his hours of service were over, he would shut himself up in his room, and pass in mournful solitude the whole time he was not on duty. The First Consul, when in good humor, would joke with him upon this savage disposition, calling him Mademoiselle Hambard. "Ah, well, what were you doing there in your room all by yourself? Doubtless you were reading some poor romances, or some old books about princesses carried off and kept under guard by a barbarous giant." To which Hambard would sullenly reply, "General, you no doubt know better than I what I was doing," referring in this way to the spies by which he believed himself to be always surrounded. Notwithstanding this unfortunate disposition, the First Consul felt very kindly to him. When the Emperor went to camp at Boulogne, Hambard refused to accompany him; and the Emperor gave him, as a place of retreat, the charge of the palace of Meudon. There he showed unmistakable symptoms of insanity, and his end was lamentable. During the Hundred Days, after a conversation with the Emperor, he threw himself against a carving-knife with such violence that the blade came out two inches behind his back. As it was believed at this time that I had incurred the anger of the Emperor, the rumor went abroad that it was I who had committed suicide, and this tragic death was announced in several papers as mine.

Hebert, ordinary valet, was a very agreeable young fellow, but very timid, and was, like all the rest of the household, devotedly attached to the First Consul. It happened one day in Egypt that the latter, who had never been able to shave himself (it was I who taught him how to shave himself, as I shall relate elsewhere at length), called Hebert to shave him, in the absence of Hambard, who ordinarily discharged that duty. As it had sometimes happened that Hebert, on account of his great timidity, had cut his master's chin, on that day the latter, who held a pair of scissors in his hand, when Hebert approached him, holding his razor, said, "Take care, you scamp; if you cut me, I will stick my scissors into your stomach." This threat, made with an air of pretended seriousness, but which was in fact only a jest, such as I have seen the Emperor indulge in a hundred times, produced such an impression on Hebert, that it was impossible for him to finish his work. He was seized with a convulsive trembling, the razor fell from his hand, and the general-in- chief in vain bent his neck, and said to him many times, laughing "Come, finish, you scamp." Not only was Hebert unable to complete his task that day, but from that time he had to renounce the duty of barber. The Emperor did not like this excessive timidity in the servants of his household; but this did not prevent him, when he restored the castle of Rambouillet, from giving to Hebert the place of concierge which he requested.

Roustan, so well known under the name of Mameluke, belonged to a good family of Georgia; carried off at the age of six or seven, and taken to Cairo, he was there brought up among the young slaves who attended upon the mamelukes, until he should be of sufficient age to enter this warlike militia. The Sheik of Cairo, in making a present to General Bonaparte of a magnificent Arab horse, had given him at the same time Roustan and Ibrahim, another mameluke, who was afterwards attached to the service of Madame Bonaparte, under the name of Ali. It is well known that Roustan became an indispensable accompaniment on all occasions when the Emperor appeared in public. He was with him in all his expeditions, in all processions, and, which was especially to his honor, in all his battles. In the brilliant staff which followed the Emperor he shone more than all others by the richness of his Oriental costume; and his appearance made a decided impression, especially upon the common people and in the provinces. He was believed to have great influence with the Emperor; because, as credulous people said, Roustan had saved his master's life by throwing himself between him and the saber of an enemy who was about to strike him. I think that this belief was unfounded, and that the especial favor he enjoyed was due to the habitual kindness of his Majesty towards every one in his service. Besides, this favor affected in no wise his domestic relations; for when Roustan, who had married a young and pretty French girl, a certain Mademoiselle Douville, whose father was valet to the Empress Josephine, was reproached by certain journals in 1814 and 1815 with not having followed to the end of his fortunes the man for whom he had always expressed such intense devotion, Roustan replied that the family ties which he had formed prevented his leaving France, and that he could not destroy the happiness of his own household.

Ibrahim took the name of Ali when he passed into the service of Madame Bonaparte. He was of more than Arabic ugliness, and had a wicked look. I recall in this connection a little incident which took place at Malmaison, which will give an idea of his character. One day, while playing on the lawn of the chateau, I unintentionally threw him down while running; and furious at his fall, he rose up, drew his poniard, which he always wore, and dashed after me to strike me. I laughed at first, like every one else, at the accident, and amused myself by making him run; but warned by the cries of my comrades, and looking back to see how close he was, I perceived at the same time his dagger and his rage. I stopped at once, and planted my foot, with my eye fixed upon his poniard, and was fortunate enough to avoid his blow, which, however, grazed my breast. Furious in my turn, as may be imagined, I seized him by his flowing pantaloons, and pitched him ten feet into the stream of Malmaison, which was barely two feet deep. The plunge brought him at once to his senses; and besides, his poniard had gone to the bottom, which made him much less dangerous. But in his disappointment he yelled so loudly that Madame Bonaparte heard him; and as she had quite a fancy for her mameluke, I was sharply scolded. However, this poor Ali was of such an unsocial temperament that he got into difficulties with almost every one in the household, and at last was sent away to Fontainebleau, to take the place of manservant there.

I now return to our campaign. On the 13th of June the First Consul spent the night at Torre-di-Galifolo, where he established his headquarters. From the day of our entry into Milan the advance of the army had not slackened; General Murat had passed the Po, and taken possession of Piacenza; and General Lannes, still pushing forward with his brave advance guard, had fought a bloody battle at Montebello, a name which he afterwards rendered illustrious by bearing it. The recent arrival of General Desaix, who had just returned from Egypt, completed the joy of the general-in-chief, and also added much to the confidence of the soldiers, by whom the good and modest Desaix was adored. The First Consul received him with the frankest and most cordial friendship, and they remained together three consecutive hours in private conversation. At the end of this conference, an order of the day announced to the army that General Desaix would take command of the division Boudet. I heard some persons in the suite of General Desaix say that his patience and evenness of temper were rudely tried during his voyage, by contrary winds, forced delays, the ennui of quarantine, and above all by the bad conduct of the English, who had kept him for some time a prisoner in their fleet, in sight of the shores of France, although he bore a passport, signed by the English authorities in Egypt, in consequence of the capitulation which had been mutually agreed upon. Consequently his resentment against them was very ardent; and he regretted much, he said, that the enemy he was about to fight was not the English.

In spite of the simplicity of his tastes and habits, no one was more ambitious of glory than this brave general. All his rage against the English was caused by the fear that he might not arrive in time to gather new laurels. He did indeed arrive in time, but only to find a glorious death, alas, so premature!

It was on the fourteenth that the celebrated battle of Marengo took place, which began early in the morning, and lasted throughout the day. I remained at headquarters with all the household of the First Consul, where we were almost within range of the cannon on the battlefield. Contradictory news constantly came, one report declaring the battle completely lost, the next giving us the victory. At one time the increase in the number of our wounded, and the redoubled firing of the Austrian cannon, made us believe that all was lost; and then suddenly came the news that this apparent falling back was only a bold maneuver of the First Consul, and that a charge of General Desaix had gained the battle. But the victory was bought at a price dear to France and to the heart of the First Consul. Desaix, struck by a bullet, fell dead on the field; and the grief of his soldiers serving only to exasperate their courage, they routed, by a bayonet charge, the enemy, who were already shaken by the brilliant cavalry charge of General Kellermann. The First Consul slept upon the field of battle, and notwithstanding the decisive victory that he had gained, was very sad, and said that evening, in the presence of Hambard and myself, many things which showed the profound grief he experienced in the death of General Desaix. He said, "France has lost one of her bravest defenders, and I one of my best friends; no one knew how much courage there was in the heart of Desaix, nor how much genius in his head." He thus solaced his grief by making to each and all a eulogy on the hero who had died on the field of honor.

"My brave Desaix," he further said, "always wished to die thus;" and then added, almost with tears in his eyes, "but ought death to have been so prompt to grant his wish?"

There was not a soldier in our victorious army who did not share so just a sorrow. Rapp and Savary, the aides-de-camp of Desaix, remained plunged in the most despairing grief beside the body of their chief, whom they called their father, rather to express his unfailing kindness to them than the dignity of his character. Out of respect to the memory of his friend, the general-in-chief, although his staff was full, added these two young officers in the quality of aides-de-camp.

Commandant Rapp (for such only was his rank at that time) was then, as he has ever been, good, full of courage, and universally beloved. His frankness, which sometimes bordered on brusqueness, pleased the Emperor; and I have many times heard him speak in praise of his aide-de-camp, whom he always styled, "My brave Rapp." Rapp was not lucky in battle, for he rarely escaped without a wound. While thus anticipating events, I will mention that in Russia, on the eve of the battle of La Moskwa, the Emperor said, in my presence, to General Rapp, who had just arrived from Dantzic, "See here, my brave fellow, we will beat them to-morrow, but take great care of yourself. You are not a favorite of fortune."—"That is," said the general, "the premium to be paid on the business, but I shall none the less on that account do my best."

Savary manifested for the First Consul the same fervid zeal and unbounded devotion which had attached him to General Desaix; and if he lacked any of the qualities of General Rapp, it was certainly not bravery. Of all the men who surrounded the Emperor, no one was more absolutely devoted to his slightest wishes. In the course of these memoirs, I shall doubtless have occasion to recall instances of this unparalleled enthusiasm, for which the Duke de Rovigo I was magnificently rewarded; but it is just to say that he did not bite the hand which rewarded him, and that he gave to the end, and even after the end, of his old master (for thus he loved to style the Emperor) an example of gratitude which has been imitated by few.

A government decree, in the month of June following, determined that the body of Desaix should be carried to the Hospice of St. Bernard, and that a tomb should be erected on that spot, in the country where he had covered himself with immortal glory, as a testimonial to the grief of France, and especially that of the First Consul.

CHAPTER V

The victory of Marengo had rendered the conquest of Italy certain. Therefore the First Consul, thinking his presence more necessary at Paris than at the head of his army, gave the command in chief to General Massena, and made preparations to repass the mountains. On our return to Milan, the First Consul was received with even more enthusiasm than on his first visit.

The establishment of a republic was in accordance with the wishes of a large number of the Milanese; and they called the First Consul their Savior, since he had delivered them from the yoke of the Austrians. There was, however, a party who detested equally these changes, the French army which was the instrument of them, and the young chief who was the author. In this party figured a celebrated artist, the singer Marchesi.

During our former visit, the First Consul had sent for him; and the musician had waited to be entreated, acting as if he were much inconvenienced, and at last presented himself with all the importance of a man whose dignity had been offended. The very simple costume of the First Consul, his short stature, thin visage, and poor figure were not calculated to make much of an impression on the hero of the theater; and after the general-in-chief had welcomed him cordially, and very politely asked him to sing an air, he replied by this poor pun, uttered in a tone the impertinence of which was aggravated by his Italian accent: "Signor General, if it is a good air which you desire, you will find an excellent one in making a little tour of the garden." The Signor Marchesi was for this fine speech immediately put out of the door, and the same evening an order was sent committing the singer to prison. On our return the First Consul, whose resentment against Marchesi the cannon of Marengo had doubtless assuaged, and who thought besides that the penance of the musician for a poor joke had been sufficiently long, sent for him again, and asked him once more to sing; Marchesi this time was modest and polite, and sang in a charming manner. After the concert the First Consul approached him, pressed his hand warmly, and complimented him in the most affectionate manner; and from that moment peace was concluded between the two powers, and Marchesi sang only praises of the First Consul.

At this same concert the First Consul was struck with the beauty of a famous singer, Madame Grassini. He found her by no means cruel, and at the end of a few hours the conqueror of Italy counted one conquest more.

> The following day she breakfasted with the First Consul and General Berthier in the chamber of the First Consul. General Berthier was ordered to provide for the journey of Madame Grassini, who was carried to Paris, and attached to the concert-room of the court.

The First Consul left Milan on the 24th; and we returned to France by the route of Mont Cenis, traveling as rapidly as possible. Everywhere the Consul was received with an enthusiasm difficult to describe. Arches of triumph had been erected at the entrance of each town, and in each canton a deputation of leading citizens came to make addresses to and compliment him. Long ranks of young girls, dressed in white, crowned with flowers, bearing flowers in their hands, and throwing flowers into the carriage of the First Consul, made themselves his only escort, surrounded him, followed him, and preceded him, until he had passed, or as soon as he set foot on the ground wherever he stopped.

The journey was thus, throughout the whole route, a perpetual fete; and at Lyons it amounted to an ovation, in which the whole town turned out to meet him. He entered, surrounded by an immense crowd, amid the most noisy demonstrations, and alighted at the hotel of the Celestins. In the Reign of Terror the Jacobins had spent their fury on the town of Lyons, the destruction of which they had sworn; and the handsome buildings which ornamented the Place Belcour had been leveled to the ground, the hideous cripple Couthon, at the head of the vilest mob of the clubs, striking the first blow with the hammer. The First Consul detested the Jacobins, who, on their side, hated and feared him; and his constant care was to destroy their work, or, in other words, to restore the ruins with which they had covered France. He thought then, and justly too, that he could not better respond to the affection of the people of Lyons, than by promoting with all his power the rebuilding of the houses of the Place Belcour; and before his departure he himself laid the first stone. The town of Dijon gave the First Consul a reception equally as brilliant.

Between Villeneuve-le-Roi and Sens, at the descent to the bridge of Montereau, while the eight horses, lashed to a gallop, were bearing the carriage rapidly along (the First Consul already traveled like a king), the tap of one of the front wheels came off. The inhabitants who lined the route, witnessing this accident, and foreseeing what would be the result, used every effort to stop the postilions, but did not succeed, and the carriage was violently upset. The First Consul received no injury; General Berthier had his face slightly scratched by the windows, which were broken; and the two footmen, who were on the steps, were thrown, violently to a distance, and badly wounded. The First Consul got out, or rather was pulled out, through one of the doors. This occurrence made no delay in his journey; he took his seat in another carriage immediately, and reached Paris with no other accident. The night of the 2d of July, he alighted at the Tuileries; and the next day, as soon as the news of his return had been circulated in Paris, the entire population filled the courts and the garden. They pressed around the windows of the pavilion of Flora, in the hope of catching a glimpse of the savior of France, the liberator of Italy.

That evening there was no one, either rich or poor, who did not take delight in illuminating his house or his garret. It was only a short time after his arrival at Paris that the First Consul learned of the death of General Kleber. The poniard of Suleyman had slain this great captain the same day that the cannon of Marengo laid low another hero of the army of Egypt. This assassination caused the First Consul the most poignant grief, of which I was an eyewitness, and to which I can testify; and, nevertheless, his calumniators have dared to say that he rejoiced at an event, which, even considered apart from its political relations, caused him to lose a conquest which had cost him so much, and France so much blood and expense. Other miserable wretches, still more stupid and more infamous, have even gone so far as to fabricate and spread abroad the report that the First Consul had himself ordered the assassination of his companion in arms, whom he had placed in his own position at the head of the army in Egypt. To these I have only one answer to make, if it is necessary to answer them at all; it is this, they never knew the Emperor.

After his return, the First Consul went often with his wife to Malmaison, where he remained sometimes for several days. At this time it was the duty of the valet de chambre to follow the carriage on horseback. One day the First Consul, while returning to Paris, ascertained a short distance from the chateau that he had forgotten his snuff-box, and sent me for it. I turned my bridle, set off at a gallop, and, having found the snuff-box on his desk, retraced my steps to overtake him, but did not succeed in doing so till he had reached Ruelle. Just as I drew near the carriage my horse slipped on a stone, fell, and threw me some distance into a ditch. The fall was very severe; and I remained stretched on the ground, with one shoulder dislocated, and an arm badly bruised. The First Consul ordered the horses stopped, himself gave orders to have me taken up, and cautioned them to be very careful in moving me; and I was borne, attended by-him, to the barracks of Ruelle, where he took pains before continuing his journey to satisfy himself that I was in no danger. The physician of his household was sent to Ruelle, my shoulder set, and my arm dressed; and from there I was carried as gently as possible to Malmaison, where, good Madame, Bonaparte had the kindness to come to see me, and lavished on me every attention.

The day I returned to service, after my recovery, I was in the antechamber of the First Consul as he came out of his cabinet. He drew near me, and inquired with great interest how I was. I replied that, thanks to the care taken of me, according to the orders of my excellent master and mistress, I was quite well again. "So much the better," said the First Consul. "Constant, make haste, and get your strength back. Continue to serve me well, and I will take care of you. Here," added he, placing in my hand three little crumpled papers, "these are to replenish your wardrobe;" and he passed on, without listening to the profuse thanks which, with great emotion, I was attempting to express, much more for the consideration and interest in me shown by him than for his present, for I did not then know of what it consisted. After he passed on I unrolled my papers: they were three bank-bills, each for a thousand francs! I was moved to tears by so great a kindness. We must remember that at this period the First Consul was not rich, although he was the first magistrate of the republic. How deeply the remembrance of this generous deed touches me, even to-day. I do not know if details so personal to me will be found interesting; but they seem to me proper as evidence of the true character of the Emperor, which has been so outrageously misrepresented, and also as an instance of his ordinary conduct towards the servants of his house; it shows too, at the same time, whether the severe economy that he required in his domestic management, and of which I will speak elsewhere, was the result, as has been stated, of sordid avarice, or whether it was not rather a rule of prudence, from which he departed willingly whenever his kindness of heart or his humanity urged him thereto.

I am not certain that my memory does not deceive me in leading me to put in this place a circumstance which shows the esteem in which the First Consul held the brave soldiers of his army, and how he loved to manifest it on all occasions. I was one day in his sleeping-room, at the usual hour for his toilet, and was performing that day the duties of chief valet, Hambard being temporarily absent or indisposed, there being in the room, besides the body servants, only the brave and modest Colonel Gerard Lacuee, one of the aides-de-camp of the First Consul. Jerome Bonaparte, then hardly seventeen years of age, was introduced. This young man gave his family frequent cause of complaint, and feared no one except his brother

Napoleon, who reprimanded, lectured, and scolded him as if he had been his own son. There was a question at the time of making him a sailor, less with the object of giving him a career, than of removing him from the seductive temptations which the high position of his brother caused to spring up incessantly around his path, and which he had little strength to resist. It may be imagined what it cost him to renounce pleasures so accessible and so delightful to a young man. He did not fail to protest, on all occasions, his unfitness for sea-service, going so far, it is said, that he even caused himself to be rejected by the examining board of the navy as incompetent, though he could easily have prepared himself to answer the few questions asked. However, the will of the First Consul must be obeyed, and Jerome was compelled to embark. On the day of which I have spoken, after some moments of conversation and scolding, still on the subject of the navy, Jerome said to his brother, "Instead of sending me to perish of ennui at sea, you ought to take me for an aide-de-camp."—"What, take you, greenhorn," warmly replied the First Consul; "wait till a ball has furrowed your face and then I will see about it," at the same time calling his attention to Colonel Lacuee, who blushed, and dropped his eyes to the floor like a young girl, for, as is well known, he bore on his face the scar made by a bullet. This gallant colonel was killed in 1805 before Guntzbourg; and the Emperor deeply regretted his loss, for he ways one of the bravest and most skillful officers of the army.

It was, I believe, about this time that the First Consul conceived a strong passion for a very intelligent and handsome young woman, Madame D. Madame Bonaparte, suspecting this intrigue, showed jealousy; and her husband did all he could to allay her wifely suspicions. Before going to the chamber of his mistress he would wait until every one was asleep in the chateau; and he even carried his precautions so far as to go from his room to hers in his night-dress, without shoes or slippers. Once I found that day was about to break before his return; and fearing scandal, I went, as the First Consul had ordered me to do in such a case, to notify the chambermaid of Madame D. to go to her mistress and tell her the hour. It was hardly five minutes after this timely notice had been given, when I saw the First Consul returning, in great excitement, of which I soon learned the cause. He had discovered, on his return, one of Madame Bonaparte's women, lying in wait, and who had seen him through the window of a closet opening upon the corridor. The First Consul, after a vigorous outburst against the curiosity of the fair sex, sent me to the young scout from the enemy's camp to intimate to her his orders to hold her tongue, unless she wished to be discharged without hope of return. I do not know whether I added a milder argument to these threats to buy her silence; but, whether from fear or for compensation, she had the good sense not to talk. Nevertheless, the successful lover, fearing another surprise, directed me to rent in the Allee des Ireuves a little house where he and Madame D. met from time to time. Such were, and continued to be, the precautions of the First Consul towards his wife. He had the highest regard for her, and took all imaginable care to prevent his infidelities coming to her knowledge. Besides, these passing fancies did not lessen the tenderness he felt for her; and although other women inspired him with love, no other woman had his confidence and friendship to the same extent as Madame Bonaparte. There have been a thousand and one calumnies repeated of the harshness and brutality of the First Consul towards women. He was not always gallant, but I have never seen him rude; and, however singular it may seem after what I have just related, he professed the greatest veneration for a wife of exemplary conduct, speaking in admiring terms of happy households; and he did not admire cynicism, either in morals or in language. When he had any liaisons he kept them secret, and concealed them with great care.

CHAPTER VI

The 3d Nivose, year IX. (Dec. 21, 1800),

> [Under the Republican regime the years were counted from the proclamation of the Republic, Sept. 22, 1792. The year was divided into twelve months of thirty days each, re-named from some peculiarity, as Brumaire (foggy); Nivose (snowy); Thermidor (hot); Fructidor (fruit), etc.; besides five supplementary days of festivals, called 'sans-culottides'. The months were divided into three decades of ten days instead of weeks, the tenth day (decadi) being in lieu of Sunday. The Republican calendar lasted till Jan. 1, 1806, as to the years and months at least, though the Concordat had restored the weeks and Sabbaths.—TRANS.]

the Opera presented, by order, The Creation of Haydn; and the First Consul had announced that he would be present, with all his household, at this magnificent oratorio. He dined on that day with Madame Bonaparte, her daughter, and Generals Rapp, Lauriston, Lannes, and Berthier. I was on duty; but as the First Consul was going to the Opera, I knew that I should not be needed at the chateau, and resolved, for my part, to go to the Feydeau, occupying the box which Madame Bonaparte allowed us, and which was situated under hers. After dinner, which the First Consul bolted with his usual rapidity, he rose from the table, followed by his officers, with the exception of General Rapp, who remained with Madame Josephine and Hortense. About seven o'clock the First Consul entered his carriage with Lannes, Berthier, and Lauriston, to go to the Opera. When they arrived in the middle of Rue Sainte-Nicaise, the escort who preceded the carriage found the road obstructed by a cart, which seemed to be abandoned, and on which a cask was found fastened strongly with ropes. The chief of the escort had this cart removed to the side of the street; and the First Consul's coachman, whom this delay had made impatient, urged on his horses vigorously, and they shot off like lightning. Scarcely two seconds had passed when the barrel which was on the cart burst with a frightful explosion. No one of the escort or of the companions of the First Consul was slain, but several were wounded; and the loss among the residents in the street and the passers-by near the horrible machine was much greater. More than twenty of these were killed, and more than sixty seriously wounded. Trepsat, the architect, had his thigh broken. The First Consul afterwards decorated him, and made him the architect of the Invalides, saying that he had long enough been the most invalid of architects. All the panes of glass at the Tuileries were broken, and many houses thrown down. All those of the Rue Sainte-Nicaise, and even some in the adjacent streets, were badly damaged, some fragments being blown into the house of the Consul Cambaceres. The glass of the First Consul's carriage was shivered to fragments. By a fortunate chance, the carriages of the suite, which should have been immediately behind that of the First Consul, were some distance in the rear, which happened in this way: Madame Bonaparte, after dinner, had a shawl brought to wear to the opera; and when it came, General Rapp jestingly criticised the color, and begged her to choose another. Madame Bonaparte defended her shawl, and said to the general that he knew as much about criticising a toilet as she did about attacking a fort. This friendly banter continued for some moments; and in the interval, the First Consul, who never waited, set out in advance, and the miserable assassins and authors of the conspiracy set fire to the infernal machine. Had the coachman of the First Consul driven less rapidly, and thereby been two seconds later, it would have been all over with his master; while, on the other hand, if Madame Bonaparte had followed her husband promptly, it would have been certain death to her and all her suite.

It was, in fact, the delay of an instant which saved her life, as well as that of her daughter, her sister-in-law, Madame Murat, and all who were to accompany them, since the carriage of these ladies, instead of being immediately behind that of the First Consul, was just leaving the Place Carrousel, when the machine exploded. The glass was shivered; and though Madame Bonaparte received no injury except the terrible fright, Hortense was slightly wounded in the face by a piece of glass, and Madame Caroline Murat, who was then far advanced in pregnancy, was so frightened that it was necessary to carry her back to the Tuileries. This catastrophe had its influence, even on the health of her child; for I have been told that Prince Achille Muratz is subject, to this day, to frequent attacks of epilepsy. As is well known, the First Consul went on to the opera, where he was received with tumultuous acclamations, the immobility of his countenance contrasting strongly with the pallor and agitation of Madame Bonaparte's, who had feared not so much for herself as for him. The coachman who had driven the First Consul with such good fortune was named Germain. He had followed him in Egypt, and in a skirmish had killed an Arab, with his own hand, under the eyes of the general-in-chief, who, struck with his courage, had cried out, "Diable! that's a brave man, he is a Caesar." The name had clung to him. It has been said that this brave man was drunk at the time of this explosion; but this is a mistake, which his conduct under the circumstances contradicts in the most positive manner. When the First Consul, after he became Emperor, went out, incognito, in Paris, it was Caesar who was his escort, without livery. It is said in the Memorial de Sainte Helene that the Emperor, in speaking of Caesar, stated that he was in a complete state of intoxication, and took the noise of the explosion for an artillery salute, nor did he know until the next day what had taken place. This is entirely untrue, and the Emperor was incorrectly informed in regard to his coachman. Caesar drove the First Consul very rapidly because he had been ordered to do so, and because he considered his honor interested in not allowing the obstacle which the infernal machine placed in his way before the explosion to delay him. The evening of the event I saw Caesar, who was perfectly sober, and he himself related to me part of the details that I have just given. A few days after, four or five hundred hackney-coachmen clubbed together to honor him, and gave him a magnificent dinner at twenty-four francs per head.

While the infernal plot was being executed, and costing the lies of many innocent citizens, without attaining the object the assassins proposed, I was, as I have said, at the Theatre Feydeau, where I had prepared myself to enjoy at my leisure an entire evening of freedom, amid the pleasures of the stage, for which I had all my life a great liking. Scarcely had I seated myself comfortably, however, when the box-keeper entered in the greatest excitement, crying out, "Monsieur Constant, it is said that they have just blown up the First Consul; there has been a terrible explosion, and it is asserted that he is dead." These terrible words were like a thunderbolt-to me. Not knowing what I did, I plunged down-stairs, and, forgetting my hat, ran like mad to the chateau. While crossing Rue Vivienne and the Palais Royal, I saw no extraordinary disturbance; but in Rue Sainte Honore there was a very great tumult, and I saw, borne away on litters, many dead and wounded, who had been at first carried into the neighboring houses of Rue Sainte Nicaise. Many groups had formed, and with one voice all were cursing the still unknown authors of this dastardly attempt. Some accused the Jacobins of this, because three months before they had placed the poniard in the hands of Cerrachi, of Arena, and of Topino Lebrun; whilst others, less numerous perhaps, thought the aristocrats, the Royalists, could alone be guilty of this atrocity. I could give no time to these various accusations, except as I was detained in forcing my way through an immense and closely packed crowd, and as rapidly as possible went on, and in two seconds was at the Carrousel. I threw myself against the wicket, but the two sentinels instantly crossed bayonets before my breast. It was useless to cry out that I was valet de chambre of the First Consul; for my bare head, my wild manner, the disorder, both of my dress and ideas, appeared to them suspicious, and they refused energetically and very obstinately to allow me to enter. I then begged them to send for the gatekeeper of the chateau; and as soon as he came, I was admitted, or rather rushed into the chateau, where I learned what had just happened. A short time after the First Consul arrived, and was immediately surrounded by his officers, and by all his household, every one present being in the greatest state of anxiety. When the First Consul alighted from his carriage he appeared calm and smiling; he even wore an air of gayety. On entering the vestibule he said to his officers, rubbing his hands, "Well, sirs, we made a fine escape! "They shuddered with indignation and anger. He then entered the grand saloon on the ground floor, where a large number of counselors of state and-dignitaries had already assembled; but hardly had they begun to express their congratulations, when he interrupted them, and in so vehement a manner that he was heard outside the saloon. We were told that after this council he had a lively altercation with Fouche, Minister of Police, whom he reproached with his ignorance of this plot, openly accusing the Jacobins of being the authors.

That evening, on retiring, the First Consul asked me laughingly if I was afraid. "More than you were, my general," I replied; and I related to him how I had heard the fatal news at the Feydeau, and had run without my hat to the very wicket of the Carrousel, where the sentinels tried to prevent my entering. He was amused at the oaths and abusive epithets with which they had accompanied their defense of the gate, and at last said to me, "After all, my dear Constant, you should not be angry with them; they were only obeying orders. They are brave men, on whom I can rely." The truth is, the Consular Guard was at this period no less devoted than it has been since as the Imperial Guard. At the first rumor of the great risk which the First Consul had run, all the soldiers of that faithful band had gathered spontaneously in the court of the Tuileries.

After this melancholy catastrophe, which carried distress into all France, and mourning into so many families, the entire police were actively engaged in searching for the authors of the plot. The dwelling of the First Consul was first put under surveillance, and we were incessantly watched by spies, without suspecting it. All our walks, all our visits, all our goings and comings, were known; and attention was especially directed to our friends, and even our liaisons. But such was the devotion of each and all to the person of the First Consul, such was the affection that he so well knew how to inspire in those around him, that not one of the persons attached to his service was for an instant suspected of having a hand in this infamous attempt. Neither at this time, nor in any other affair of this kind, were the members of his household ever compromised; and never was the name of the lowest of his servants ever found mixed up in criminal plots against a life so valued and so glorious.

The minister of police suspected the Royalists of this attempt; but the First Consul attributed it to the Jacobins, because they were already guilty, he said, of crimes as odious. One hundred and thirty of the most noted men of this party were transported on pure suspicion, and without any form of trial. It is now known that the discovery, trial, and execution of Saint Regent and Carbon, the true criminals, proved that the conjectures of the minister were more correct than those of the chief of state.

The 4th Nivose, at noon, the First Consul held a grand review in the Place Carrousel, where an innumerable crowd of citizens were collected to behold, and also to testify their affection for his person, and their indignation against the enemies who dared attack him only by assassination. Hardly had he turned his horse towards the first line of grenadiers of the Consular Guard, when their innumerable acclamations rose on all sides. He rode along the ranks, at a walk, very slowly, showing his appreciation, and replying by a few simple and affectionate words to this effusion of popular joy; and cries of "Vive Bonaparte! Vive the First Consul!" did not cease till after he had re-entered his apartments.

The conspirators who obstinately persisted, with so much animosity, in attacking the life of the First Consul, could not have chosen a period in which circumstances would have been more adverse to their plans than in 1800 and 1801, for then the Consul was beloved not only for his military deeds, but still more for the hope of peace that he gave to France, which hope was soon realized. As soon as the first rumor spread abroad that peace had been concluded with Austria, the greater part of the inhabitants of Paris gathered under the windows of the Pavilion of Flora. Blessings and cries of gratitude and joy were heard on all sides; then musicians assembled to give a serenade to the chief of state, and proceeded to form themselves into orchestras; and there was dancing the whole night through. I have never seen a sight more striking or more joyous than the bird's-eye view of this improvised jubilee.

When in the month of October, the, peace of Amiens having been concluded with England, France found herself delivered from all the wars that she had maintained through so many years, and at the cost of so many sacrifices, it would be impossible to form an idea of the joy which burst forth on all sides. The decrees which ordered either the disarmament of vessels of war, or the placing of the forts on a peace footing, were welcomed as pledges of happiness and security. The day of the reception of Lord Cornwallis, Ambassador of England, the First Consul ordered that the greatest magnificence should be displayed. "It is necessary," he had said the evening before, "to show these proud Britons that we are not reduced to beggary." The fact is, the English, before setting foot on the French continent, had expected to find only ruins, penury, and misery. The whole of France had been described to them as being in the most distressing condition, and they thought themselves on the point of landing in a barbarous country. Their surprise was great when they saw how many evils the First Consul had already repaired in so short a time, and all the improvements that he still intended to carry out; and they spread through their own country the report of what they themselves called the prodigies of the First Consul, by which thousands of their compatriots were influenced to come and judge with their own eyes. At the moment that Lord Cornwallis entered the great hall of the Ambassadors with his suite, the eyes of all the English must have been dazzled by the sight of the First Consul, surrounded by his two colleagues, with all the diplomatic corps, and with an already brilliant military court.

In the midst of all these rich uniforms, his was remarkable for its simplicity; but the diamond called the Regent, which had been put in pawn under the Directory, and redeemed a few days since by the First Consul, sparkled on the hilt of his sword.